# THE STORY OF LEO THE LION

By Blanche Roesser

## Gareth Stevens
PUBLISHING

leveled reader
science

**Please visit our website, www.garethstevens.com. For a free color catalog of all our high-quality books, call toll free 1-800-542-2595 or fax 1-877-542-2596.**

**Library of Congress Cataloging-in-Publication Data**

Roesser, Blanche, author.
  The story of Leo the lion / Blanche Roesser.
     pages cm. — (Stories in the stars)
  Includes bibliographical references and index.
  ISBN 978-1-4824-2673-1 (pbk.)
  ISBN 978-1-4824-2674-8 (6 pack)
  ISBN 978-1-4824-2675-5 (library binding)
  1. Heracles (Greek mythological character)—Juvenile literature. 2. Hercules (Roman mythological character)—Juvenile literature. 3. Nemean lion (Greek mythology)—Juvenile literature. 4. Constellations—Folklore—Juvenile literature. 5. Mythology, Greek—Juvenile literature. I. Title.
  BL820.H5R64 2016
  292.1'3—dc23

                                    2014050360

Published in 2016 by
**Gareth Stevens Publishing**
111 East 14th Street, Suite 349
New York, NY 10003

Copyright © 2016 Gareth Stevens Publishing

Designer: Nicholas Domiano
Editor: Therese Shea

Photo credits: Cover, pp. 1, 21 (Leo the Lion) Daniel Pyne/Dorling Kindersley/Getty Images; cover, p. 1 (stars) nienora/Shutterstock.com; p. 5 AlexanderZam/Shutterstock.com; p. 7 Vladimir Korostyshevskiy/Shutterstock.com; p. 9 LTL/Universal Images Group/Getty Images; p. 11 DEA PICTURE LIBRARY/De Agostini Picture Library/Getty Images; p. 13 Matyas Rehak/Shutterstock.com; p. 15 DEA/G. DAGLI ORTI/De Agostini Picture Library/Getty Images; p. 17 Solodov Alexey/Shutterstock.com; p. 19 Yganko/Shutterstock.com.

Printed in the United States of Ameri  **3 2872 50127 1906**

CPSIA compliance information: Batch #CS15GS: For further information contact Gareth Stevens, New York, New York at 1-800-542-2595.

# CONTENTS

**Boldface** words appear in the glossary.

## Meet Leo

A group of stars that forms a shape is called a constellation. Leo the Lion is one of the most famous constellations. Many **ancient** peoples have written about these stars. *Leo* means "lion" in Latin.

5

# The Labors of Hercules

Many people connect the Leo constellation to the Nemean (NEE-mee-uhn) Lion. This scary animal was in **myths** about a great hero. He's called Hercules (HUHR-kyuh-leez) in Roman myths. Hercules was half god and the strongest man on Earth.

Hercules

7

Hercules was hated by the queen of the gods, Juno. She made him go **insane** and kill his family. As **punishment**, he had to work for a king who hated him. The king gave Hercules 12 impossible jobs, or labors.

Juno

9

# The Nemean Lion

The first labor was to kill the Nemean Lion. It hunted in the hills around an area called Nemea and ate people. This was no ordinary lion. No **weapons** could hurt it. Hercules set out for Nemea and began to track the beast.

11

Hercules found the lion. He tried to shoot it with arrows. Then, he tried to use his club. However, these weapons weren't powerful enough against the magical animal. But Hercules didn't give up. He followed the lion to its cave.

13

The lion's cave had two doors. Hercules blocked one of them so the lion couldn't get away. He picked up the lion in his arms and **wrestled** it. Some say he lost a finger fighting it. Finally, Hercules choked the lion to death.

No weapons could harm the Nemean Lion. However, Hercules's strong arms did! The hero is often shown in artwork wearing a lion's skin. Some say this was the Nemean Lion's hide. Hercules took the dead lion back to the king.

17

Hercules completed 11 more impossible jobs. He went on to kill other nasty beasts, such as a nine-headed snake and man-eating birds. He had other **adventures**, too. There's also a constellation named after Hercules!

Hercules constellation

19

## Look Up for Leo

Since Earth moves around the sun, we can't always see Leo the Lion. In the Northern **Hemisphere**, we see the constellation starting in March each year. It's easy to see in April and May. When it's spring, look up for Leo!

21

# GLOSSARY

**adventure:** an exciting or dangerous event

**ancient:** coming from a time long past

**hemisphere:** one-half of Earth

**insane:** having a serious illness of the mind

**myth:** a story that was told by an ancient people to explain something

**punishment:** the act of making someone suffer for a crime or for bad behavior

**weapon:** something used to cause injury or death

**wrestle:** to fight by gripping, holding, and pushing rather than hitting

# FOR MORE INFORMATION

## BOOKS

Forest, Christopher. *The Kids' Guide to the Constellations.* Mankato, MN: Capstone Press, 2012.

Galat, Joan Marie. *Dot to Dot in the Sky: Stories of the Zodiac.* North Vancouver, BC, Canada: Walrus Books, 2007.

McCaughrean, Geraldine. *Hercules.* Chicago, IL: Cricket Books, 2005.

## WEBSITES

### Leo Constellation: Facts About the Lion
*www.space.com/16845-leo-constellation.html*
Read about the constellation and its brightest stars.

### Leo? Here's Your Constellation
*earthsky.org/constellations/leo-heres-your-constellation*
Find out how to spot Leo in the night sky.

# INDEX